The
Second Amendment

Preserving the Inalienable Right of
Individual Self-Protection

David Barton

Aledo, Texas
www.wallbuilders.com

The Second Amendment: Preserving the Inalienable Right of Individual Self-Protection
Copyright © 2000, David Barton
1st Edition, 7th Printing, 2020

Additional materials available from:
WallBuilders
P. O. Box 397
Aledo, TX 76008
(817) 441-6044
www.wallbuilders.com

Cover Painting:
Battle of Lexington, April 19, 1775. Oil on canvas by William Barnes Wollen (1857-1936), 1910.

Courtesy of the Director, National Army Museum, London

Cover Design:
Jeremiah Pent
Lincoln-Jackson

ISBN 10: 0-925279-77-3
ISBN 13: 978-0-925279-77-4

Printed in the United States of America

Table of Contents

The Second Amendment

*Preserving the Inalienable Right of
Individual Self-Protection*

The Second Amendment has become one of the most controversial parts of the Constitution. That Amendment, written in 1789 by the First Congress and ratified in 1791 by the States as part of the original Bill of Rights, states:

A well regulated militia being necessary to the security of a free state, the right of the people to keep and bear arms shall not be infringed.

The meaning of the right "to keep and bear arms," and the segment of the citizenry to which that right applies, has been heatedly and vociferously debated in recent years. Specifically, what does "people" mean? Does "people" refer to the collective body (the "militia") or does "people" refer to every citizen individually?

While gun rights supporters assert that the right to keep and bear arms is an individual right like the freedom of speech or religion, gun opponents assert that the right pertains only to collective bodies (e.g., the military, police, National Guard, etc.) and not to individuals. According to gun opponents:

> [T]here is *no* individual right to bear arms in the Bill of Rights. [1] *USA Today* (emphasis added)

> [L]aw-abiding Americans have *no* unconditional right to firearms access. [2] *New York Post* (emphasis added)

> The debate over gun control offers a revealing case study of the misuse of the Constitution. . . . [T]he idea that the Bill of Rights guarantees each individual a right to own a gun. . . . [is] a constitutional illusion. [3] *The San Francisco Barrister*

> [T]he sale, manufacture, and possession of handguns ought to be banned. . . . [W]e do not believe the 2nd Amendment guarantees an individual right to keep them. [4] *The Washington Post*

[T]here is *no* Constitutional guarantee for private ownership of firearms. [5] *Austin American Statesman* (emphasis added)

Believing that the Constitution offers no protection for individual gun ownership, gun opponents therefore encourage efforts to restrict or ban citizen access to firearms, particularly handguns. They frequently utilize highly-publicized, tragic instances of violence (such as those at Columbine, Fort Worth, Seattle, etc.) to bolster their argument that guns should be left only in the hands of "professionals." For example:

There is no reason for anyone in the country, for anyone except a police officer or a military person, to buy, to own, to have, to use, a handgun. [6] *Michael Gartner, former president of NBC News*

[T]he Second Amendment . . . protects only the right to "bear arms" for the purpose of service in the "militia," and . . . *not* . . . firearm ownership unrelated to militia service. [7] *Statement filed by fifty-two law professors and historians in a Second Amendment lawsuit* (emphasis added)

[T]he individual's right to bear arms applies only to the preservation or efficiency of a "well-regulated militia." Except for lawful police and military purposes, the possession of weapons by individuals is *not* constitutionally protected. [8] *The ACLU* (emphasis added)

One of the few things on which both gun rights supporters and gun rights opponents agree is that law enforcement officials, the militia, and the military do have the right to keep and bear arms. Therefore, this work will examine the contested scope of the Second Amendment: do individual citizens have a constitutionally-protected right "to keep and bear arms"? Four sources of information will be examined to determine the answer: (1) America's earliest legal commentaries, (2) the writings of the Founding Fathers, (3) early State laws, and (4) State constitutions.

These four categories of information will indisputably demonstrate that a citizen's right to keep and bear arms is an individually guaranteed right and that efforts to restrict or regulate gun possession by ordinary law-abiding citizens – no matter what "humanitarian" or alleged "historical" arguments might undergird such efforts – are unequivocal violations of the explicit protections and original intentions of the Constitution. In fact, after examining the historical documents and records surrounding the framing of the Second Amendment, if any individual or group still claims that the right to keep and bear arms is not an individual right, then that individual or group is just as likely – to use the words of nineteenth-century military chaplain William Biederwolf – to "look all over the sky at high noon on a cloudless day and not see the sun." [9]

I. Early Legal Commentaries

Among the many sources which indicate the original intent, and thus the proper interpretation, of the Second Amendment are early legal commentaries. Examining these commentaries (which often contain the legal writings which influenced the framing of the Second Amendment as well as the writings of those who drafted that Amendment) is vital to understanding the reasoning behind and scope of protection intended by that Amendment.

In fact, a common error in constitutional interpretation is the failure to examine a document according to its original meaning. As explained by Noah Webster (the Founder responsible for Article I, Section 8, ¶ 8 of the Constitution), not only misinterpretation but even serious error can result when original meanings are ignored:

[I]n the lapse of two or three centuries, changes have taken place which . . . obscure the sense of the original languages. . . . The effect of these changes is that some words are . . . now used in a sense different from that which they had . . . [and thus] present a wrong signification or false ideas. Whenever words are understood in a sense different from that which they had when introduced. . . . mistakes may be very injurious. [10]

To avoid such "injurious mistakes," President Thomas Jefferson admonished Supreme Court Justice William Johnson:

On every question of construction, carry ourselves back to the time when the Constitution was adopted, recollect the spirit manifested in the debates, and instead of trying what meaning may be squeezed out of the text, or invented against it, conform to the probable one in which it was passed. [11]

Constitution signer James Madison agreed with this approach, stating:

I entirely concur in the propriety of resorting to the sense in which the Constitution was accepted and ratified by the nation. In that sense *alone* it is the *legitimate* Constitution. And if that be not the guide in expounding it, there can be no security for a consistent and stable, more than for a faithful, exercise of its powers. . . . What a metamorphosis would be produced in the code of law if all its ancient phraseology were to be taken in its modern sense. [12] (emphasis added)

James Wilson, an original Justice on the Supreme Court, similarly exhorted:

The first and governing maxim in the interpretation of a statute is to discover the meaning of those who made it. [13]

Justice Joseph Story (appointed to the Supreme Court by President James Madison) also emphasized this principle, declaring:

The first and fundamental rule in the interpretation of all [documents] is to construe them according to the sense of the terms and the intention of the parties. [14]

The following excerpts from legal commentaries written both before and after the adoption of the Constitution and its Second Amendment establish the understanding of the rights addressed by that Amendment at the time it was framed. As will be demonstrated, the Second Amendment was to protect what was frequently called "the first law of nature" – the right of self-protection. This right of self-protection was, in fact, considered an inalienable right – a right guaranteed to every citizen individually.

However, before establishing that the Second Amendment was intended to secure an individual's right "to keep and bear arms" as an inalienable right, it is important to establish just what an inalienable right is. Constitution signer John Dickinson, like many of the others in his day, defined an inalienable right as a right "which God gave to you and which no inferior power has a right to take away." [15]

Our Founders believed that it was the duty of government to protect inalienable, or God-granted, rights from encroachment or usurpation. This was made clear by James Wilson.

James Wilson was one of only six Founders who signed both the Declaration of Independence and the Constitution; he was the second most-active member of the Constitutional Convention, speaking 168 times on the floor of the Convention; he was a law professor; he was nominated by President George Washington as an original Justice to the U.S. Supreme Court; and in 1792, he was coauthor of America's first legal commentaries on the Constitution. [16] Wilson helped lay the foundation for a purely American system of jurisprudence and started the first organized system

of legal training in America. [17] In fact, James Wilson conducted his legal training for students while simultaneously sitting as a Justice on the Supreme Court.

Wilson taught his students that the specific protections found in our government documents did not create new rights but rather secured old rights – that our documents were merely . . .

> . . . to acquire a new security for the possession or the recovery of those rights to . . . which we were *previously entitled* by the immediate gift or by the unerring law of our all-wise and all-beneficent Creator. [18] (emphasis added)

Wilson then asserted that . . .

> . . . every government which has not this in view as its principal object is not a government of the legitimate kind. [19]

John Adams agreed, declaring that:

> *Rights* [are] antecedent to all earthly government; *Rights* . . . cannot be repealed or restrained by human laws; *Rights* [are] derived from the great Legislator of the universe. [20]

Thomas Jefferson similarly explained that government . . .

> . . . is to declare and enforce only our *natural rights* and duties and to take *none* of them from us. [21] (emphasis added)

The Second Amendment (as well as the other Amendments) did not grant or bestow any new right on citizens; rather, it simply recognized and provided, in the words of James Wilson, "a new security" to the already existing, natural, God-given rights of citizens for their own self-defense. As Alexander Hamilton affirmed:

> [T]he Supreme Being gave existence to man, together with the *means of preserving* and beautifying that existence. He ... invested him [man] with an *inviolable right* to personal liberty and *personal safety*. [22] (emphasis added)

Since the right to self-defense was an inalienable personal right, the Second Amendment simply assured each citizen that he would have the tools necessary to defend his life, family, or property from aggression, whether from an individual or a government. That the Second Amendment simply secured in writing a right which God had already conferred on His creation was confirmed in the legal commentaries that undergirded American law. †

---

† Although much less emphasized during the framing of the Second Amendment, gun activities related to hunting were also covered under the protections of that Amendment since it was also considered to be a natural, God-given right for each individual to be able to provide food for his table through what Pennsylvania in 1787 described as "killing game." [23]

One such commentary was *Blackstone's Commentaries on the Laws*, the most influential legal commentary at the time of the framing of the Second Amendment. Originally introduced in America in 1766 while America was still a British colony, *Blackstone's* eventually became *the* standard for American attorneys and judges. In fact, Thomas Jefferson observed that American lawyers used *Blackstone's* with the same dedication and reverence that Muslims used the Koran. [24] Concerning the right of citizens to own and use arms, *Blackstone's* declared:

> The . . . right of the [citizens] that I shall at present mention, is that of having arms for their defense. . . . [This is] the natural right of resistance and self-preservation when the sanctions of society and laws are found insufficient to restrain the violence of oppression. . . . [T]o vindicate these rights when actually violated or attacked, the [citizens] are entitled, in the first place, to the regular administration and free course of justice in the courts of law; next, to the right of petitioning the [government] for redress of grievances; and lastly, to the right of having and using arms for self-preservation and defense. [25]

Not only did the Second Amendment secure what Blackstone had called "the right of having and using arms" for "the natural right of resistance and self-preservation" but our Founders further believed that it was a *duty* for every citizen to be willing to exercise that right when necessary. This was made clear by James Wilson, who declared:

Homicide is enjoined [required] when it is necessary for the defense of one's person or house. . . . [I]t is the great natural law of self-preservation which, as we have seen, cannot be repealed or superseded or suspended by any human institution. This law, however, is expressly recognized in the constitution of Pennsylvania: "The *right* of the citizens *to bear arms in the **defense of themselves** shall not be questioned.*" . . . [E]very man's house is deemed, by the law, to be his castle; and the law, while it invests him with the power, [places] on him the duty of the commanding officer [of his house]. "Every man's house is his castle . . . and if any one be robbed in it, it shall be esteemed his own default and negligence." [26] (emphasis added)

Zephaniah Swift, author of America's first legal text in 1792, similarly confirmed:

[S]elf-defense, or self-preservation, is one of the first laws of nature, which no man ever resigned upon entering into society. [27]

Another legal commentary addressing the fundamental rights recognized in the Second Amendment was that of St. George Tucker. Tucker, an attorney and a military officer wounded twice during the American Revolution, was one of the leaders of the 1786 Annapolis Convention that led to the convening of the Constitutional Convention in 1787. Tucker became one of the most distinguished legal scholars in early America, serving as a law professor in the College of William and Mary, a justice on the Virginia Supreme Court, and as a federal judge under President James Madison. Tucker, however, was perhaps most famous for his annotated edition of *Blackstone's Commentaries*. In that celebrated work, Tucker declared:

> The right of self defence is the first law of nature: in most governments it has been the study of rulers to confine this right within the narrowest limits possible. Wherever . . . the right of the people to keep and bear arms is, under any color or pretext whatsoever, prohibited, liberty, if not already annihilated, is on the brink of destruction. [28]

A concurring view is presented in the legal commentary authored by William Rawle. Rawle was offered (but declined) a federal judgeship by President

George Washington and instead accepted from him the position of a U.S. Attorney. Rawle later founded an early legal society that became a law academy. In 1825, he published his *View of the Constitution,* one of America's first extensive commentaries on the Constitution. That work became an early classic, serving as a textbook in numerous legal institutions as well as in the U.S. Military Academy. In his commentary, Rawle explained:

> In the Second [Amendment], it is declared. . . . that "the right of the people to keep and bear arms shall not be infringed." The prohibition is general. No clause in the Constitution could, by *any* rule of construction, be conceived to give the Congress a power to disarm the people. A flagitious [flagrantly wicked] attempt could only be made under some general pretense by a State legislature. But if, in any blind pursuit of inordinate power, either [the State or federal government] should attempt it, this Amendment may be appealed to as a restraint on both. [29] (emphasis added)

The year after Rawle released his work, an even more comprehensive legal commentary was published by Chancellor James Kent. Kent is recognized by historians and scholars as one of the two "Fathers of American Jurisprudence," sharing that honor with Supreme Court Justice Joseph Story. Kent had embarked on the practice of law after reading *Blackstone's Commentaries* during the American Revolution; and during the Constitutional Convention of 1787, he became a close friend of many of the delegates. He subsequently became a law professor and a justice on the New York Supreme Court, where he instituted the practice of handing down written opinions. In 1826, Kent issued his *Commentaries on American Law,* still considered today as a "foremost American institutional legal treatise." [30] In fact, Supreme Court Justice Lewis Powell (1907-1998) declared of Kent's commentaries that, "One who desires a brief review of the foundation stones of our constitutional jurisprudence can go nowhere else with such profit." [31] In those commentaries, Kent declared:

> The municipal law of our . . . country has likewise left with *individuals* the exercise of the natural right of self-defense. . . . The right of self-defense . . . is founded in the law of nature, and is not, and *cannot* be, superseded by the law of society. [32] (emphasis added)

Perhaps the most authoritative legal commentary ever written on the U.S. Constitution was that of

Joseph Story. Story was the son of one of the "Indi-ans" at the Boston Tea Party; he was the founder of Harvard Law School; he was called the "foremost of American legal writers"; [33] he was nominated to the U.S. Supreme Court by President James Madison; and he is the youngest Justice ever appointed to the Court. During his 34 years on the Court, Story authored 286 opinions, of which ninety-four percent were recorded as the Court's opinion. Story was one of America's most prolific judicial writers, and – along with James Kent – is titled a "Father of American Jurisprudence." In his 1833 *Commentaries on the United States Constitution*, Justice Story declared:

> The next amendment is: "A well-regulated militia being necessary to the security of a free state, the right of the people to keep and bear arms shall not be infringed." The importance of this article will scarcely be doubted by any persons who have duly reflected upon the subject. . . . The right of the citizens to keep and bear arms has justly been considered as the palladium of the liberties of a republic since it offers a strong moral check against the usurpation and arbitrary power of rulers; and will generally, even if these are successful in the first instance, enable the people to resist and triumph over them. . . . There is certainly

no small danger that indifference may lead to disgust, and disgust to contempt, and thus gradually undermine all the protection intended by this clause of our national Bill of Rights. [34]

(Justice Story here asserts that which will be reconfirmed in subsequent sections: that the scope of the Second Amendment allowed citizens to defend themselves not only against the aggression of other individuals but also against that of government – "against the usurpation and arbitrary power of rulers.")

Henry St. George Tucker (son of St. George Tucker mentioned earlier) was another distinguished legal scholar. Serving as a soldier in the War of 1812 and afterwards as a U.S. Congressman, he became the Chancellor of a law school and spent 17 years as a judge. In his 1844 legal lectures, Tucker reaffirmed what his legal predecessors had already declared:

[T]he law of self-preservation. . . . is indeed familiarly styled the first law of nature. . . . [It] is recognized, *sub modo,* by the laws of every civilized country. . . . The right of self-defense, (and with it of self-preservation), may, without danger of controversy, therefore be laid down as the first law of nature. Nor is it . . . lost by entering into society. [35]

Another significant legal commentary was that
of John Randolph Tucker. Tucker was dean of a law
school, a constitutional law professor, the Attorney
General of Virginia, and the President of the American Bar Association. In 1899, Tucker authored his
two-volume commentaries on the Constitution. In
those commentaries, Tucker explained:

> The Second Amendment reads thus: "A well
> regulated militia being necessary to the secu-
> rity of a free State, the right of the people to
> keep and bear arms shall not be infringed."
> This prohibition indicates that the security
> of liberty against the tyrannical tendency of
> government is only to be found in the right of
> the people to keep and bear arms in resisting
> the wrongs of government. [36]

Clearly, legal commentaries and commentators
across the centuries agreed: there was an inherent,
natural right of self-defense and self-preservation of
which the "right to keep and bear arms" was intrinsic,
belonging to every individual. In fact, the Senate
Judiciary Committee has even noted:

> The proposal [for the wording of the Second
> Amendment] finally passed the House in its
> present form: "A well regulated militia, being
> necessary to the security of a free state the right
> of the people to keep and bear arms, shall not be

infringed." In this form it was submitted into the Senate, which passed it the following day. The Senate in the process indicated its intent that the right be an *individual* one, for *private* purposes, by *rejecting* an amendment which would have limited the keeping and bearing of arms to bearing "for the common defense".... The conclusion is thus inescapable that the history, concept, and wording of the Second Amendment to the Constitution of the United States, as well as its interpretation by every major commentator and court in the first half-century after its ratification, indicates that what is protected is an *individual* right of a *private citizen* to own and carry fire-arms in a peaceful manner. [37] (emphasis added)

II. Views of the Founding Fathers

Another important source for establishing the scope and protections of the Second Amendment is the declarations of those Founding Fathers under whose watchful eye both the government and the Second Amendment were created. Those Founders confirm that every citizen not only has a right to life, liberty, and property but also the natural right to use force to preserve and defend those rights. Notice some of their emphatic declarations on this subject:

Resistance to sudden violence for the preservation not only of my person, my limbs, and life, but of my property, is an indisputable right of nature which I never surrendered to the public by the compact of society and which, perhaps, I could not surrender if I would. . . . [T]he maxims of the law and the precepts of Christianity are precisely coincident in relation to this subject. [38] JOHN ADAMS, U.S. PRESIDENT, SIGNER OF THE DECLARATION, ONE OF THE TWO SIGNERS OF THE BILL OF RIGHTS

Among the natural rights of the Colonists are these: first, a right to life; secondly, to liberty; thirdly, to property – together with the right to support and defend them in the best manner they can. [39] SAMUEL ADAMS, SIGNER OF THE DECLARATION, "FATHER OF THE AMERICAN REVOLUTION"

[T]he said Constitution [should] be never construed . . . to prevent the people of the United States, who are peaceable citizens, from keeping their own arms. [40] SAMUEL ADAMS, SIGNER OF THE DECLARATION, "FATHER OF THE AMERICAN REVOLUTION"

The right . . . of bearing arms . . . is declared to be inherent in the people. [41] FISHER AMES, A FRAMER OF THE SECOND AMENDMENT IN THE FIRST CONGRESS

The great object is that every man be armed. . . . Every one who is able may have a gun. But have we not learned by experience that, necessary as it is to have arms, . . . it is still far from being the case? [42] PATRICK HENRY, GOVERNOR, PATRIOT LEADER

Guard with jealous attention the public liberty. Suspect every one who approaches that jewel. Unfortunately, nothing will preserve it but downright force. Whenever you give up that force, you are inevitably ruined. [43] PATRICK HENRY, GOVERNOR, PATRIOT LEADER

[M]ankind must be prepared and fitted for the reception, enjoyment, and preservation of universal permanent peace before they will be blessed with it. Are they as yet fitted for it?

Certainly not. Even if it was practicable, would it be wise to disarm the good before "the wicked cease from troubling?" [Job 3:17] [44] JOHN JAY, ORIGINAL CHIEF-JUSTICE, U.S. SUPREME COURT

And what country can preserve its liberties if its rulers are not warned from time to time that this people preserve the spirit of resistance? Let them take arms. [45] THOMAS JEFFERSON, U.S. PRESIDENT, SIGNER OF THE DECLARATION

No [citizen] shall be debarred the use of arms within his own lands. [46] THOMAS JEFFERSON, U.S. PRESIDENT, SIGNER OF THE DECLARATION

The people are not to be disarmed of their weapons. They are left in full possession of them. . . . This is a principle which secures religious liberty most firmly. [47] ZECHARIAH JOHNSTON, REVOLUTIONARY SOLDIER, VIRGINIA LEGISLATOR, RATIFIER OF THE U.S. CONSTITUTION

[T]o preserve liberty, it is essential that the whole body of the people always possess arms, and be taught alike, especially when young, how to use them. [48] RICHARD HENRY LEE, SIGNER OF THE DECLARATION, A FRAMER OF THE SECOND AMENDMENT IN THE FIRST CONGRESS

[T]he advantage of being armed [is an advantage which] the Americans possess over the people of almost every other nation. . . . [I]n the several kingdoms of Europe . . . the governments are afraid to trust the people with arms. [49] JAMES MADISON, U.S. PRESIDENT, SIGNER OF THE CONSTITUTION, A FRAMER OF THE SECOND AMENDMENT IN THE FIRST CONGRESS

Forty years ago, when the resolution of enslaving America was formed in Great-Britain, the British parliament was advised . . . to disarm the people. That it was the best and most effectual way to enslave them. But that they should not do it openly; but to weaken them and let them sink gradually. [50] GEORGE MASON, DELEGATE TO THE CONSTITUTIONAL CONVENTION, "FATHER OF THE BILL OF RIGHTS"

I consider and fear the natural propensity of rulers to oppress the people. I wish only to prevent them from doing evil. . . . Divine providence has given to every individual the means of self-defense. [51] GEORGE MASON, DELEGATE TO THE CONSTITUTIONAL CONVENTION, "FATHER OF THE BILL OF RIGHTS"

I am thus far a Quaker [a pacifist]: I would gladly agree with all the world to lay aside the use of arms and settle matters by negotiation; but unless the whole will, the matter ends, and I take up my musket and thank Heaven

He has put it in my power. [52] THOMAS PAINE,
PATRIOT, AUTHOR

[A]rms, like laws, discourage and keep the in-
vader and the plunderer in awe, and preserve order in the world as well as property. The balance
of power is the scale of peace. The
same balance would be preserved
were all the world destitute of
arms, for all would be alike; but
since some will not, others dare
not lay them aside. . . . The history
of every age and nation establishes
these truths, and facts need but
little arguments when they prove themselves. [53]
THOMAS PAINE, PATRIOT, AUTHOR

A people who mean to continue free must be
prepared to meet danger in person, not to rely
upon the fallacious protection of . . . armies. [54]
EDMUND RANDOLPH, DELEGATE TO THE CON-
STITUTIONAL CONVENTION, SECRETARY OF STATE
UNDER PRESIDENT GEORGE WASHINGTON

It [is] a chimerical idea to suppose that a country like this could ever be enslaved. How is an
army for that purpose to. . . . subdue a nation
of freemen who know how to prize liberty and
who have arms in their hands? [55] THEODORE

Sedgwick, revolutionary soldier, a framer of the second amendment in the first congress

A free people ought . . . to be armed. [56] George Washington, u.s. president, signer of the constitution

[N]o man should scruple or hesitate a moment to use arms in defense. [57] George Washington, u.s. president, signer of the constitution

Before a standing army can rule, the people must be disarmed – as they are in almost every kingdom in Europe. The supreme power in America cannot enforce unjust laws by the sword because the whole body of the people are armed. [58] Noah Webster, revolutionary soldier, legislator, responsible for article i, section 8, ¶ 8 of the constitution

The declarations of those who framed our government and its Second Amendment confirm that the rights in that Amendment indeed secure the Divine right of individual citizens to use whatever force or arms may be necessary to preserve the other rights given to them by God and protected by the Constitution.

In fact, a work jointly authored in 1825 by William Sumner (a military general from Massachusetts) and Alden Partridge (a captain, a military instructor at

West Point, and the founder of Norwich University) observed that citizens's blessings of "having the choice of their leaders, the firesides, the temples of justice, the altars of religion, national independence and glory, which, under Providence, we have built up, will continue in permanent security" only so long as "people are trained to the use of arms and keep them in their hands." [59]

III. Early Legislative Acts

The views held by early Americans on the Second Amendment right "to keep and bear arms" were a reflection of the views previously established by experience and decades of tradition and finally incorporated by law into their own States. Those early laws provide the third source which affirms that the right "to keep and bear arms" pertains to every individual citizen.

Consider, for example, a 1623 Virginia law that prevented a citizen from traveling unless he was "well armed." [60] And in 1631, Virginia required:

> That men go not to work . . . without their arms. All men that are fitting to bear arms shall bring their pieces to the church, [and] upon pain of every offense . . . pay 2 lb of tobacco. [61]

In 1658, Virginia required every householder to have a functioning firearm within his house; and in

1673, the law provided that a citizen who claimed that he was too poor to purchase a firearm would have one purchased for him by the government, which would then require him to pay a reasonable price when

able to do so. [62] And a 1676 law declared that "Liberty is granted to all persons to carry their arms wheresoever they go." [63]

The New Plymouth Colony in 1632 required that "each person . . . have piece, powder, and shot; a sufficient musket or other serviceable piece. . . . [and] be at all times furnished with two pounds of powder and ten pounds of bullets." [64] In fact, so serious was this Colony about its citizens bearing arms that it established the following fines for those who were not armed:

The fines of such as are defective in their arms:

For such as are wholly defective: 10 shillings
    that want a piece: 6 shillings
    that want a sword: 2 shillings
    that want powder: 5 shillings
    that want bullets: 2 shillings. [65]

In 1639, the Newport Colony required that "none shall come to any public meeting without his weapon." [66]

In 1650, Connecticut ordered that its citizens "be always provided with, and have in readiness by them, half a pound of powder, two pound of serviceable bullets or shot, and two fathom of match to every matchlock, upon the penalty of five shillings a month for each person's default herein." [67]

And Georgia felt it necessary in 1770, "for the better security of the inhabitants," to require every resident "to carry firearms to places of public worship." [68]

Not only do these early laws recognize the right of every citizen to keep and bear arms, they further reveal that every private individual citizen was considered a part of the public defense. As explained by Richard Henry Lee, a signer of the Declaration and an original framer of the Second Amendment:

[T]he militia shall always . . . include, *according to the past and general usage of the States*, all men capable of bearing arms. [69] (emphasis added)

(Examples of State constitutions confirming this declaration will be presented shortly.)

For this reason, "militia" in the Second Amendment was understood to be every individual citizen rather than just the army or the organized military:

A militia . . . are in fact the people themselves. . . . [and] are for the most part employed at home in their private concerns. [70] RICHARD HENRY LEE, SIGNER OF THE DECLARATION, A FRAMER OF THE SECOND AMENDMENT IN THE FIRST CONGRESS

The militia . . . are . . . the people at large. [71] TENCH COXE, ATTORNEY GENERAL OF PENNSYLVANIA, ASSISTANT SECRETARY OF THE TREASURY UNDER PRESIDENT GEORGE WASHINGTON

The militia is composed of free citizens. [72] SAMUEL ADAMS, SIGNER OF THE DECLARATION, "FATHER OF THE AMERICAN REVOLUTION"

Who are the militia? They consist now of the whole people. [73] GEORGE MASON, DELEGATE TO THE CONSTITUTIONAL CONVENTION, "FATHER OF THE BILL OF RIGHTS"

It was not surprising, therefore, that when the United States Congress passed the first federal law on this subject (the Militia Act of 1792), it defined "militia of the United States" not as the Continental Army or any other organized military body but rather as including almost every adult male in the United States. Under that act, each adult was required – *by law* – to possess a firearm and a minimum supply of ammunition and military equipment, [74] and this law continued in force into the twentieth century. In fact, the *current* law still states, "The militia of the United States consists of *all* able-bodied males at least 17 [and] under 45 years of age." [75]

Significantly, numerous State constitutions adopted subsequent to the Second Amendment and the Militia Act of 1792 contain similar declarations. For example:

> The militia shall consist of all able-bodied male persons.
>
> ALABAMA, 1867; [76] 1875; [77] ARKANSAS, 1868; [78] 1874; [79] COLORADO, 1876; [80] FLORIDA, 1868; [81] 1885; [82] GEORGIA, 1868; [83] IDAHO, 1889; [84] ILLINOIS, 1818; [85] 1870; [86] INDIANA, 1851; [87] IOWA, 1846; [88] 1857; [89] KANSAS, 1855; [90] 1857; [91] 1858; [92] 1859; [93] KENTUCKY, 1850; [94] 1890; [95] LOUISIANA, 1868; [96] MAINE, 1819; [97] MARYLAND, 1864; [98] MICHIGAN, 1850; [99] MISSISSIPPI, 1868; [100] 1890; [101] MISSOURI, 1861; [102] 1865; [103] 1875; [104] MONTANA, 1889; [105] NEW YORK, 1894; [106] NORTH CAROLINA, 1868; [107] 1876; [108] NORTH DAKOTA, 1889; [109] OHIO, 1851; [110] OREGON, 1857; [111] SOUTH CAROLINA, 1868; [112] 1895; [113] SOUTH DAKOTA, 1889; [114] UTAH, 1895; [115] VIRGINIA, 1870; [116] WASHINGTON, 1889; [117] WYOMING, 1889 [118]

(Significantly, each of these States has its own State National Guard unit and its own separate laws regulating that body. The above militia provision, however, is separate from those laws and pertains not to the National Guard but rather to individual "able-bodied persons" outside that body.)

Thus, the State constitutions (both colonial and modern), the federal Constitution, early federal laws, and especially the declarations of those who framed the Second Amendment all confirm that the guarantees of the U. S. Constitution concerning the right to keep and bear arms were always understood to be inclusive of and extended to *every* "able-bodied citizen."

Furthermore, the federal Constitution was not formed in a vacuum, independent of the influence of the States. That is, it cannot reasonably be argued that the Second Amendment established a concept touching the right of citizen self-protection contrary to that which existed throughout the nation at that time. It is irrefutable that the views held by the States on this issue had significant impact on the drafting of the federal Second Amendment. In fact, simply consider how the Bill of Rights – including the Second Amendment – came into existence.

While the Constitutional Convention ended with a proposal for a new federal government, it closed on a somewhat divisive tone. During the Convention, George Mason had moved that a Bill of Rights be added to the Constitution to provide specific protection for States and individuals, [119] but others at the Convention opposed any Bill of Rights, and their position prevailed. [120] For this reason, Convention delegates such as George Mason, Elbridge Gerry, and Edmund Randolph refused to sign the new Constitution.

These delegates returned to their home States to lobby against the ratification of the Constitution until a Bill of Rights was added. As a result of their voices (and numerous others in the States who agreed with them), the ratification of the Constitution almost failed in Virginia, [121] Massachusetts, [122] New Hampshire, [123] and New York. [124] Rhode Island adamantly refused to ratify it, [125] and North Carolina refused to do so until limitations were placed upon the federal government.[126] Although the Constitution was eventually ratified, a clear message had been delivered: there was strong sentiment demanding the inclusion of a Bill of Rights. †

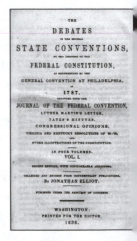

---

† The best source for examining the call for a Bill of Rights in the various State conventions is Elliot's *Debates in the Several State Conventions on the Adoption of the Federal Constitution* (1836). This is the original compilation of the records from each State's ratifying convention, and even today this work remains a primary reference, unrivaled in both scholarship and accuracy.

When the First Congress convened, Elbridge Gerry (a signer of the Declaration of Independence and one of the members of the Constitutional Convention who had refused to sign the Constitution) reminded the other Members:

> The ratification of the Constitution in several States would never have taken place had they not been assured that the[ir] objections would have been duly attended to by Congress. And I believe many members of these conventions would never have voted for it if they had not been persuaded that Congress would notice them with that candor and attention which their importance requires. [127]

Congress, therefore, did pay close attention to what the States had proposed, and did deliberate upon and create a Bill of Rights which addressed the concerns raised by the States. It is instructive to examine the suggested wording on the right to keep and bear arms which was sent to the federal government by the States who offered their suggestions for a Bill of Rights. † For example, New Hampshire's proposed wording was:

† Significantly, every State which submitted a proposal for a Bill of Rights included specific protection for the right to keep and bear arms. However, proposals to protect free speech and other rights appeared in only some of the proposals, thus indicating that the general consensus among the people was that the right to keep and bear arms was even more important than many other individual rights.

Congress shall never disarm any citizen. [128]

And in the Massachusetts Convention, wording had been proposed declaring:

[T]hat the said Constitution be never construed . . . to prevent the people of the United States, who are peaceable citizens, from keeping their own arms. [129]

While New Hampshire and Massachusetts had specifically addressed only the individual right to keep and bear arms, Pennsylvania went further, proposing:

[N]o law shall be passed for disarming the people, or any of them. [130]

An important point is made in the Pennsylvania proposal: not only did its wording make clear that the right to be armed was applicable to the collective group ("the people") but it also applied equally to every individual ("or *any* of them"). Proposals from other States confirm their desire that there should be both a collective *and* an individual right to keep and bear arms.

For example, the proposals from Virginia, New York, and Rhode Island included one clause to protect individuals, followed by a dividing semicolon, followed by a separate clause to protect the militia:

That the people have a right to keep and bear arms; that a well-regulated militia, composed of the body of the people trained to arms, is the proper, natural, and safe defence of a free state. [131]

It is not surprising, then, that in 1789, Albert Gallatin (one of the framers of Pennsylvania's proposals for the Bill of Rights, a U.S. Representative and Senator under President George Washington, and the Secretary of the Treasury for Presidents Jefferson and Madison) declared:

The whole of that Bill [of Rights] is a declaration of the rights of the people at large or considered as individuals.... [I]t establishes ... rights of the *individual* as inalienable. [132] (emphasis added)

Indeed, when one examines the Bill of Rights, it is seen that *each* of the Amendments offers to every citizen a protection of his or her *individual* rights against potential abuse or intrusion by the government. [†] For example, the First Amendment gives individual citizens a protection of their speech and religious expression from the control of government; the Second Amendment, of their own self-defense against tyrannical individuals or governments; the Third, the sanctity of their homes against governmental military intrusion;

---

† While the federal Bill of Rights afforded to citizens protection of their individual rights from intrusive federal powers, each State's Bill of Rights had already afforded to citizens – well before the federal Bill of Rights – similar individual protections against intrusive State powers.

the Fourth, the protection of their persons and property against unreasonable searches or seizures by the government's police powers; the Fifth and Sixth, the preservation of their due-process legal rights against overly aggressive judicial powers; the Seventh, of their right to be judged by their own peers rather than by government officials; and the Eighth, their right to be protected against government tortures. The final two Amendments, the Ninth and the Tenth, simply reiterated that the government was not to encroach on any of the other individual rights retained by the people or the States. Very simply, *each* of the Amendments in the Bill of Rights afforded specific *individual* protections to every citizen.

In fact, Fisher Ames, an original framer of the Bill of Rights and of the Second Amendment in the First Congress, affirmed this view when he declared that . . .

. . . if a Bill of rights is violated, there every injured citizen may expect, and will have more complete re-dress, than an army of insurgents could give him. No act can have the force of law against the Bill of Rights. Every farmer ought to read it and learn its nature and value. He will prize it more than his acres; for without it, another might reap where he sows. [133]

Thomas Jefferson similarly affirmed this view when, in a letter supporting the Bill of Rights, he told James Madison:

[A] Bill of Rights is what the people are entitled to against every government on earth, general or particular; and what no just government should refuse. [134]

James Madison acknowledged that this was indeed the sentiment behind the movement for a Bill of Rights, telling Jefferson that:

[A]mong the advocates for the Constitution, there are some who wish for further guards to public liberty and *individual rights*. As far as these may consist of a constitutional declaration of the most essential rights, it is probable that they will be added. [135] (emphasis added)

And when the Bill of Rights was finally introduced by James Madison in the First Congress, Madison reminded the other Members:

I believe that the great mass of the people who opposed it [the Constitution] disliked it because it did not contain effectual provisions against encroachments on particular rights. . . . But whatever may be the form which the several

States have adopted in making declarations in favor of particular rights, the great object in view is to limit and qualify the powers of government by excepting out of the grant of power those cases in which the government ought not to act. . . . [E]very government should be disarmed of powers which trench upon those particular rights. [136]

Each Amendment was to protect an individual right; and to some of those Amendments were also added a protection on collective rights (e.g., of the people to assemble, of the militia, of juries, etc.). Based, therefore, on the individual protections appearing in each Amendment, it is illogical to assert – as do gun control proponents – that the Second Amendment should be the only Amendment not to protect an individual right. Clearly, the records prove otherwise.

In fact, James Madison originally proposed that the right to keep and bear arms appear as a textual amendment to be inserted in the Constitution in Article I, Section 9 in the section limiting Congress' power over individual citizens (e.g., outlawing the suspension of habeas corpus, bills of attainder, ex post facto laws, etc.). [137] Based on his own proposal, Madison clearly viewed the right to keep and bear arms as an individual citizen's civil right.

IV. State Constitutions

Because the Second Amendment was primarily a reflection of the belief present in the individual States, the State constitutions are the fourth source that affirm that "the right to keep and bear arms" was universally understood to be an individual right. In fact, State constitutions adopted even a century-and-a-half *after* the Second Amendment still continued to reflect the original understanding. The following clauses are reflective of many others found in State constitutions on this subject:

Through Divine goodness, *all* men have, by nature, the rights of . . . enjoying and *defending* life and liberty [and] of acquiring and *protecting* reputation and property. (emphasis added)

DELAWARE, 1792; [138] DELAWARE, 1831 [139]

All men are . . . endowed by their Creator with certain inalienable rights, among which are the rights of enjoying and *defending* their lives and liberties, [and] of acquiring, possessing, and *protecting* property. (emphasis added)

SOUTH CAROLINA, 1868 [140]

All persons have certain natural, essential, and inalienable rights, among which may be reckoned the right of enjoying and *defending* their lives and liberties; [and] of acquiring, possessing, and *protecting* property. (emphasis added)

ARKANSAS, 1836; [141] 1874; [142] CALIFORNIA, 1849; [143] COLORADO, 1876; [144] FLORIDA, 1838;[145] 1868; [146] 1885; [147] IDAHO, 1889; [148] ILLINOIS, 1818; [149] INDIANA, 1816; [150] IOWA, 1820; [151] KANSAS, 1855; [152] MAINE, 1819; [153] MASSACHUSETTS, 1780; [154] NEVADA, 1864; [155] NEW HAMPSHIRE, 1783; [156] 1792; [157] 1902; [158] NEW JERSEY, 1844; [159] NORTH DAKOTA, 1889; [160] PENNSYLVANIA, 1776; [161] 1790; [162] SOUTH DAKOTA, 1889; [163] UTAH, 1895; [164] VERMONT, 1777 [165]

The right of no person to keep and bear arms in defense of his home, person and property, or in aid of the civil power when thereto legally summoned, shall be called to question.

COLORADO, 1876; [166] MISSISSIPPI, 1890; [167] MISSOURI, 1875; [168] MONTANA, 1889 [169]

The people have the right to bear arms for their security and defense.

IDAHO, 1889;[170] KANSAS, 1855;[171] UTAH, 1895 [172]

Every citizen has a right to bear arms in defense of himself and the State. (emphasis added)

ALABAMA, 1819; [173] 1865; [174] 1875; [175] 1901; [176] CONNECTICUT, 1818; [177] FLORIDA, 1868; [178] 1885; [179] INDIANA, 1816; [180] 1851; [181] MICHIGAN, 1835; [182] 1850; [183] MISSISSIPPI, 1817; [184] 1833; [185] OHIO, 1802; [186] OREGON, 1857; [187] PENNSYLVANIA, 1776; [188] TEXAS, 1838; [189] 1845; [190] VERMONT, 1777; [191] 1793 [192]

The right of the people to keep and bear arms shall not be infringed.

GEORGIA, 1865; [193] 1877 [194]

The rights of the citizens to bear arms in defense of themselves and the State shall not be questioned.

KENTUCKY, 1799; [195] 1850; [196] MISSOURI, 1820; [197] PENNSYLVANIA, 1790; [198] SOUTH DAKOTA, 1889; [199] VERMONT, 1786; [200] 1793; [201] WASHINGTON, 1889; [202] WYOMING, 1889 [203]

V. Conclusions and Solutions

There can be no doubt that under the original intentions and interpretations, the guarantees of the Second Amendment were extended to every citizen individually. This has been demonstrated by legal commentaries, declarations of the Founding Fathers, early State laws, and State constitutions.

Nevertheless, an argument raised today against continuing those guarantees is that "times have changed"; therefore the original intentions of the Second Amendment should be modernized. Or, in the language of former Chief-Justice Earl Warren (1891-1974) in *Trop v. Dulles*, a constitutional Amendment . . .

. . . must draw its meaning from the *evolving standards* of decency that mark the progress of a maturing society. [204] (emphasis added)

The fact that governments *do* need to change ("evolve") and to incorporate social adjustments (i.e., the ending of slavery, the granting of suffrage to women, etc.) makes the theoretical argument to "modernize" the Second Amendment appealing to many. Yet, on serious reflection, it is not reasonable to assert that an inalienable, God-given natural right has changed and thus should be "modernized," whether it be the right to life, liberty, property, etc., or the right to protect those rights. Nevertheless, for the sake of discussion, pursue the proposition that the Second Amendment should evolve.

Interestingly, two centuries ago, the drafters of the Constitution believed that times would change and therefore so should the Constitution. However, they would have vehemently disagreed with the mechanism by which this change occurs today.

The Founders made clear that when the meaning, and thus the application, of any part of the Constitution was to be altered, it was to be at the hands of the people, not at the feet of the Court or through the encroachment of a legislative body. For this reason, Article V was placed in the Constitution to establish the proper means whereby the people might adjust, or "evolve," their government:

> The Congress, whenever two thirds of both Houses shall deem it necessary, shall propose *amendments* to this Constitution, or, on the application of the legislatures of two thirds of the several States, shall call a convention for proposing amendments.

Very simply, the *people*, through the means established in our governing documents, may add amendments to the Constitution in order to modernize it as they think necessary. It is this method of updating the Constitution that *must* be followed. As Samuel Adams forcefully declared:

[T]he *people alone* have an incontestable, unalienable, and indefeasible right to institute government and to reform, alter, or totally change the same when their protection, safety, prosperity, and happiness require it. And the federal Constitution, *according to the mode prescribed therein,* has already undergone such amendments in several parts of it as from experience has been judged necessary. [205] (emphasis added)

George Washington also warned Americans to adhere strictly to this manner of changing the meaning of the Constitution:

If, in the opinion of the people, the distribution or the modification of the constitutional powers be in any particular wrong, *let it be corrected by an* **amendment** *in the way which the Constitution designates.* But let there be no change by usurpation; for though this in one instance may be the instrument of good, it is the customary weapon by which free governments are destroyed. [206] (emphasis added)

Alexander Hamilton echoed this warning, declaring:

[The] Constitution is the standard to which we are to cling. Under its banners, bona fide [without deceit], we must combat our political foes, *rejecting all changes but through the channel itself provides for **amendments**.* [207] (emphasis added)

In short, if the meaning of the Second Amendment – and thus the scope of its protections – is to change, it must be done by the people themselves according to the process established in Article V. Any other method of change, whether by judicial decision, legislative action, deliberate misinterpretation, etc., is an illegitimate use and an abuse of powers and is a usurpation of the constitutionally-guaranteed rights of the people. Current efforts by judges, legislators, academia, and media crusaders to "upgrade" the meaning of the Second Amendment – despite any well-meaning intentions which might rest behind such efforts – are, as George Washington explained, "the customary weapon by which free governments are destroyed."

Furthermore, Supreme Court Justice Joseph Story explained why there can be no basis for arbitrarily evolving the transcendent, inalienable rights such as those secured by the Second Amendment. He declared:

There can be no freedom where there is no safety to property or personal rights. Whenever legislation . . . breaks in upon personal liberty or compels a sur- render of personal privileges, upon any pretext, plausible or otherwise, it matters little whether it be the act of the many or the few, of the solitary despot or the assembled multitude; it is still in its essence tyranny. It matters still less what are the causes of the change; rather urged on by a spirit of innovation, or popular delusion, or State necessity (as it is falsely called), it is still power, irresponsible power, against right. [208]

Allowing any small or elite group, no matter how loud they may be or how powerful they may seem, to be the determinant in the interpretation of the Constitution places America under what President Thomas Jefferson so aptly described as "the despo- tism of an oligarchy." [209]

In addition to the "times change" argument for "evolving" the Second Amendment, there is also the subjective, emotional argument. That is, since every individual with any sense of humanity detests see- ing families destroyed, innocent children sacrificed, and promising lives snuffed out as a result of gun violence, the argument is advanced that reducing the number of guns will produce a safer society.

While this argument appeals strongly to our humanitarian instincts, interestingly, our Founding Fathers explained why such an argument is fallacious. They – and subsequent generations of Americans – long understood that the key to a safe society rested not on the regulation of guns, swords, knives or any other kind of weapon but rather on the regulation of the heart, something accomplished only by the combined influence of religion and education.

They realized that although civil laws attempted to regulate and restrain outward conduct by defining norms of behavior, those laws could not address the heart, the actual source of violence and crime. According to Constitution signer Abraham Baldwin, this influence over the heart was "an influence beyond the reach of laws and punishments and can be claimed only by religion and education." [210]

As John Quincy Adams (a President, U.S. Representative, and U.S. Senator) similarly explained:

Human legislators can undertake only to prescribe the actions of men: they acknowledge their inability to govern and direct the sentiments of the heart. . . . It is one of the greatest marks of Divine favor . . . that [God] gave them rules . . . for the government of the heart. [211]

Thomas Jefferson similarly acknowledged:

> The precepts of philosophy . . . laid hold of actions only. He [Jesus] pushed His scrutinies into the heart of man, erected His tribunal in the region of his thoughts, and purified the waters at the fountain head. [212]

Consider murder as an example. Since civil law prohibits it, how can religion contribute anything more? Because religion, unlike civil statutes, addresses murder *before* it occurs – while it is still only a thought in the heart (see, for example, Matthew 5:22-28). Similarly, civil law cannot prevent hate, but religion can; and while the attitude of hate, legally speaking, is not a crime, it often leads to a crime (assault, murder, slander, etc.); and it is not the law, but religion, which successfully confronts hate and thus can prevent its crimes. Additionally, to covet is not illegal, but it, too, often results in crimes (theft, burglary, embezzlement, etc.); and only religion can prevent covetousness and thus the crimes it ultimately produces. Religion effectively provides what John Quincy Adams termed the "rules for the government of the heart" that prevent the crimes which originate internally but often manifest themselves externally in gun violence.

Notice how oft-repeated among our Founders was the emphasis that this personal, internal self-government was a direct societal benefit resulting from the combined strength of religion and education:

[W]e have no government armed with power capable of contending with human passions unbridled by morality and religion. Avarice, ambition, revenge, or gallantry [hypocrisy] would break the strongest cords of our Constitution as a whale goes through a net. Our Constitution was made only for a moral and religious people. It is wholly inadequate to the government of any other. [213] JOHN ADAMS, U.S. PRESIDENT, SIGNER OF THE DECLARATION, ONE OF THE TWO SIGNERS OF THE BILL OF RIGHTS

[T]hree points of doctrine ... form the foundation of all morality. The first is the existence of a God; the second is the immortality of the human soul; and the third is a future state of rewards and punishments.... [Let] a man ... disbelieve either of these articles of faith and that man will have no conscience, he will have no other law than that of the tiger or the shark; the laws of man may bind him in chains or may put him to death, but they never can make him wise, virtuous, or happy. [214] JOHN QUINCY ADAMS, U.S. PRESIDENT

[N]either the wisest constitution nor the wisest laws will secure the liberty and happiness of a

people whose manners are universally corrupt. [215]
SAMUEL ADAMS, SIGNER OF THE DECLARATION,
"FATHER OF THE AMERICAN REVOLUTION"

When the minds of the people in general are viciously disposed and unprincipled, and their conduct disorderly, a free government will be attended with greater confusions and evils more horrid than the wild, uncultivated state of nature. It can only be happy when the public principles and opinions are properly directed and their manners regulated. . . . by religion and education. [216]
ABRAHAM BALDWIN, SIGNER OF THE CONSTITUTION,
A FRAMER OF THE SECOND AMENDMENT IN CONGRESS

[T]he primary objects of government are the peace, order, and prosperity of society. . . . To the promotion of these objects, particularly in a republican government, good morals are essential. Institutions for the promotion of good morals are therefore objects of legislative provision and support: and among these . . . religious institutions are eminently useful and important. [217]
OLIVER ELLSWORTH, DELEGATE TO THE CONSTI-
TUTIONAL CONVENTION, A FRAMER OF THE SECOND
AMENDMENT IN CONGRESS, CHIEF-JUSTICE OF THE
U.S. SUPREME COURT

[T]he Holy Scriptures. . . . can alone secure to society, order and peace, and to our courts of justice and constitutions of government, purity, stability, and usefulness. In vain, without the Bible, we increase penal laws and draw entrenchments around our institutions. Bibles are strong entrenchments. Where they abound, men cannot pursue wicked courses. [218] JAMES McHENRY, SIGNER OF THE CONSTITUTION, SECRETARY OF WAR UNDER PRESIDENTS GEORGE WASHINGTON AND JOHN ADAMS

Without the restraints of religion . . . men become savages. [219] BENJAMIN RUSH, SIGNER OF THE DECLARATION

Let it simply be asked, "Where is the security for property, for reputation, for life, if the sense of religious obligation desert. . . ?" [220] GEORGE WASHINGTON, U.S. PRESIDENT, SIGNER OF THE CONSTITUTION

[T]he cultivation of the religious sentiment represses licentiousness, . . . inspires respect for and order, and gives strength to the whole social fabric. [221] DANIEL WEBSTER, "DEFENDER OF THE CONSTITUTION"

[T]he education of youth should be watched with the most scrupulous attention. . . . for it is much easier to introduce and establish an effectual system for preserving morals than to correct by penal statutes the ill effects of a bad system. [222] NOAH WEBSTER, REVOLUTIONARY SOLDIER, LEGISLATOR, RESPONSIBLE FOR ARTICLE I, SECTION 8, ¶ 8 OF THE CONSTITUTION

[To] promote true religion is the best and most effectual way of making a virtuous and regular people. Love to God and love to man is the substance of religion; when these prevail, civil laws will have little to do. [223] JOHN WITHERSPOON, SIGNER OF THE DECLARATION

When religious principles are neglected, disregarded, or suppressed, government then utilizes extensive manpower and expends massive financial sums attempting to restrain behavior which is the external manifestation of internal chaos and disorder. Robert Winthrop (Speaker of the U.S. House, 1847-1849) best summarized this truth when he declared:

Men, in a word, must necessarily be controlled either by a power within them or by a power without them; either by the Word of God or by the strong arm of man; either by the Bible or by the bayonet. [224]

It is little wonder, then, that basic religious teachings were long promoted throughout society and specifically incorporated into public education. As Daniel Webster noted:

> We regard it [public education] as a wise and liberal system of police by which property, and life, and the peace of society are secured. We seek to prevent in some measure the extension of the penal code by inspiring a salutary and conservative principle of virtue and of knowledge in an early age. . . . [W]e seek . . . to turn the strong current of feeling and opinion, as well as the censures of the law and the denunciations of religion, against immorality and crime. [225]

Religious teachings were considered to be such a fundamental part of a well-rounded education that the Founders feared what might transpire if education no longer included those principles. As signer of the Declaration Benjamin Rush warned:

> In contemplating the political institutions of the United States, I lament that we waste so much time and money in punishing crimes and take so little pains to prevent them. . . . [by] the universal education of our youth in the principles . . . of the Bible. [226]

Earlier generations understood that religion – which produced morality, internal restraints, and a basic knowledge of rights and wrongs – must be publicly encouraged and supported to ensure domestic tranquility and safety. In fact, a query by Patrick Henry offered two centuries ago – a query he thought farfetched at the time – seems appropriate today:

> Are we at last brought to such an humiliating and debasing degradation [loss of morals] that we cannot be trusted with arms . . . ? [227]

Experience proves that in a nation such as ours, the promotion and encouragement of religion and morality allows government to concentrate on its primary function: serving, rather than restraining. In short, the successful key to controlling gun violence is inculcating the restraint of the heart from an early age.

Yet, in addition to learning to regulate and restrain the passions of the heart, youth were also early taught gun safety. As Richard Henry Lee, a signer of the Declaration and a framer of the Second Amendment, explained:

> [I]t is essential that the whole body of the people always possess arms and be taught alike, *especially when young*, how to use them. [228] (emphasis added)

And Thomas Jefferson similarly advised his young fifteen year-old nephew:

A strong body makes the mind strong. As to the species of exercise, I advise the gun. While this gives a moderate exercise to the body, it gives boldness, enterprise, and independence to the mind. . . . Let your gun, therefore, be the constant companion of your walks. [229]

John Quincy Adams also believed that youth should early be instructed in the use of guns and proper gun safety. In fact, when he was dispatched by President James Madison as Minister to Russia, Adams left his three sons in the care of his younger brother, Thomas. After arriving in St. Petersburg, Adams wrote his brother with specific instructions regarding the training of the boys (George, age 9; John, age 7; and Charles, age 3) – especially George. Adams told his brother:

One of the things which I wish to have them taught – and which no man can teach better than you – is the use and management of firearms. This must undoubtedly be done with great caution, but it is customary among us – particularly when children are under the direction of ladies – to withhold it too much and too long from boys. The accidents which happen among children arise more frequently from their ignorance than from their misuse of weapons which they know to be dangerous. As you are a sportsman, I beg you occasionally from this time to take George out with you in your shooting excursions – teach him gradually the use of the musket, its construction, and the necessity of prudence in handling it; let him also learn the use of pistols, and exercise him at firing at a mark. [230]

Interestingly, the early years of John Quincy Adams provide a clear illustration of the training that young people received both in the governance of the heart and in the proper use of weapons. As John Quincy Adams recounted, his youthful days were during years of great stress and turmoil:

The year 1775 was the eighth year of my age. Among the first fruits of the War was the expulsion of my father's family from their peaceful abode in Boston. . . . Boston became a walled and beleaguered town. . . . For the space of twelve months, my mother with her infant children dwelt, liable every hour of the day and of the night to be butchered in cold blood or taken and carried into Boston as hostages. . . . My father was separated from his family on his way to attend the Continental Congress. And there my mother with her children lived in unintermitted danger of being consumed with them all in a conflagration kindled by a torch in the same hands which on the 17th of June lighted the fires of Charlestown. I saw with my own eyes those fires, and heard Britannia's thunders in the battle of Bunkers' Hill, and witnessed the tears of my mother and mingled with them my own at the fall of [General Joseph] Warren, a dear friend of my father and a beloved physician to me. [231]

Despite these trying circumstances, John Quincy Adams noted that his religious instruction had continued:

My mother was the daughter of a Christian clergyman, and therefore bred in the faith of deliberate detestation of war. . . . Yet, in that same spring and summer of 1775, she taught me to repeat daily, after the Lord's Prayer, before rising from bed, the *Ode of Collins* on the patriot warriors. . . . Of the impression made upon my heart by the sentiments inculcated in these beautiful effusions of patriotism and poetry you may form an estimate by the fact that now, seventy-one years after they were thus taught me, I repeat them from memory without reference to the book. [232]

And during that same period, the famous Massachusetts Minute Men, as they traveled to and from the various areas of conflict, spent many a night at the home of the Adams. On those occasions, the eight-year-old John Quincy Adams would shoulder his musket and perform for the Minute Men the various musket drills that he had learned from his father. In fact, half-a-century after the occurrence, Adams recalled that event in a conversation with one of those original Minute Men:

Mr. Cary. . . . asked me if I remembered a company of militia who, about the time of the battle of Lexington in 1775, came down from Bridgewater and passed the night at my father's house and barn, at the foot of Penn's Hill, and in the midst of whom my father placed me, then a boy between seven and eight years, and I went through the manual exercise of the musket by word of command from one of them. I told him I remembered it as distinctly as if it had been last week. He said he was one of that company. [233]

As he looked back on his early training in religion and weapons, John Quincy Adams remarked:

Do you wonder that a boy of seven years of age, who witnessed this scene, should be a patriot? [234]

Training young persons both in the handling of their heart and in the handling of weapons was long proved by experience to be the best preventive for violence. In fact, so effective was this training that New York Supreme Court Justice James Kent (1763-1847, called a "Father of American Jurisprudence") once observed that violence was so rare that during a sixteen year period on the bench he had faced only eight murder cases! [235]

The successful approach to gun safety which characterized American society for generations should be reinstated today; efforts should be abandoned to encroach upon the God-given, natural, inalienable right of individuals "to keep and bear arms" secured in the Second Amendment. ■

Endnotes

1. Richard Benedetto, "Gun Rights Are A Myth," *USA Today,* December 28, 1994.

2. "Time for Gun Control," *New York Post,* August 12, 1999.

3. Dennis Henigan, "The Right To Be Armed: A Constitutional Illusion," *The San Francisco Barrister,* December, 1989.

4. "Legal Guns Kill Too," *The Washington Post,* November 5, 1999.

5. "A History of the Second Amendment," *Austin American Statesman*, April 3, 2000.

6. Michael Gartner, former president of NBC News, "Glut of Guns: What Can We Do About Them?" *USA Today,* January 16, 1992.

7. Brief for an Ad Hoc Group of [Fifty-Two] Law Professors and Historians As Amici Curiae at 3, *United States v. Timothy Joe Emerson* (5th Cir. 1999) (No. 99-10331)

8. American Civil Liberties Union (ACLU), policy statement #47, 1996.

9. *Encyclopedia of Religious Quotations,* Frank Mead, editor (New Jersey: Fleming H. Revell Company, 1965), p. 50, quoting William Biederwolf.

10. Noah Webster, *The Holy Bible . . . with Amendments of the Language* (New Haven: Durrie & Peck, 1833), p. iii.

11. Thomas Jefferson, *Memoir, Correspondence, and Miscellanies,* Thomas Jefferson Randolph, editor (Boston: Gray and Bowen, 1830), Vol. IV, p. 373, to Judge William Johnson on June 12, 1823.

12. James Madison, *Selections from the Private Correspondence of James Madison from 1813–1836,* J. C. McGuire, editor (Washington, 1853), p. 52, to Henry Lee on June 25, 1824.

13. James Wilson, *The Works of the Honorable James Wilson,* Bird Wilson, editor (Philadelphia: Bronson and Chauncey, 1804), Vol. I, p. 14, from "Lectures on Law Delivered in the College of Philadelphia; Introductory Lecture: Of the Study of the Law in the United States."

14. Joseph Story, *Commentaries on the Constitution of the United States* (Boston: Hilliard, Gray, and Company, 1833), Vol. I, p. 383, § 400.

15. John Dickinson, *Letters from a Farmer in Pennsylvania*, R. T. H. Halsey, editor (New York: The Outlook Company, 1903), p. xlii, letter to the Society of Fort St. David's, 1768; see also John Quincy Adams, *An Oration Delivered Before the Cincinnati Astronomical Society on the Occasion of Laying the Cornerstone of an Astronomical Observatory on the 10th of November, 1843* (Cincinnati: Shepard & Co., 1843), pp. 13-14.

16. James Wilson and Thomas McKean, *Commentaries on the Constitution of the United States of America* (London: J. Debrett, 1792).

17. *Dictionary of American Biography*, s.v. "Wilson, James."

18. Wilson, *Works*, Vol. II, p. 454.

19. Wilson, *Works*, Vol. II, p. 466.

20. John Adams, *The Works of John Adams*, Charles Francis Adams, editor (Boston: Charles C. Little and James Brown, 1851), Vol. III, p. 449, from his "Dissertation on the Canon and Feudal Law," 1765.

21. Jefferson, *Memoir, Correspondence, and Miscellanies*, Vol. IV, p. 278, to Francis Gilmer on June 7, 1816.

22. Alexander Hamilton, *The Farmer Refuted: Or, A More Impartial and Comprehensive View of the Dispute Between Great Britain and the Colonies* (New York: James Rivington, 1775), p. 6.

23. A report from the 1787 Pennsylvania Convention to ratify the U.S. Constitution included protection "for killing game" as part of their suggestion for the original wording of the Second Amendment (see *The Address and Reasons of Dissent of the Minority of the Convention of Pennsylvania to their Constituents* (Boston: Powers, 1787), p. 6, Art. 7; see also *The Pennsylvania Packet, and Daily Advertiser*, December 18, 1787) and this language is subsequently found in current State constitutions, including Delaware, art. 1, § 20; Nebraska, art. 1, § 1; Nevada, art. 1; New Mexico, art. II, § 6: North Dakota, art. 1, § 1; West Virginia, art. III, § 22; Wisconsin, art. 1, § 25; etc.

24. Thomas Jefferson, *Writings of Thomas Jefferson*, Albert Bergh, editor (Washington, D. C. Thomas Jefferson Memorial Association, 1904), Vol. XII, p. 392, to Governor John Tyler on May 26, 1810.

25. William Blackstone, *Commentaries on the Laws* (Philadelphia: Robert Bell, 1771), Vol. I, pp. 143-144.

26. Wilson, *Works*, Vol. III, pp. 84-85.

27. Zephaniah Swift, *A System of the Laws of the State of Connecticut* (Windham: John Byrne, 1796), Vol. II, p 302; see also Vol. II, p. 2.

28. *Blackstone's Commentaries: With Notes and Reference*, St. George Tucker, editor (Philadelphia: William Young Birch, and Abraham Small, 1803), Vol. I, p. 300.

29. William Rawle, *A View of the Constitution of the United States of America,* second edition (Philadelphia: Philip H. Nicklin, 1829), pp. 125-126.

30. *Dictionary of American Biography,* s. v. "Kent, James."

31. *Dictionary of American Biography,* s. v. "Kent, James."

32. James Kent, *Commentaries on American Law* (New York: O. Halsted, 1827), Vol. II, p. 12, "On the Absolute Rights of Persons."

33. *Dictionary of American Biography,* s. v. "Story, Joseph."

34. Story, *Commentaries,* Vol. III, pp. 746-747, § 1889 and § 1890.

35. Henry St. George Tucker, *A Few Lectures on Natural Law* (Charlottesville: James Alexander, 1844), pp. 10-11.

36. John Randolph Tucker, *The Constitution of the United States,* Henry St. George Tucker, editor (Chicago: Callaghan & Co., 1899), Vol. II, p. 671, 25;

37. *The Right to Keep and Bear Arms,* Report of the Subcommittee on the Constitution of the Committee on the Judiciary, United States Senate, Ninety-Seventh Congress, Second Session, February, 1982, pp. 9, 17.

38. John Adams, "On Private Revenge," *Boston Gazette,* September 5, 1763.

39. Samuel Adams, *The Writings of Samuel Adams,* Harry Alonzo Cushing, editor (New York: G. P. Putnam's Sons, 1906), Vol. II, p. 351, from "The Rights Of The Colonists, A List of Violations Of Rights and A Letter Of Correspondence, Adopted by the Town of Boston, November 20, 1772," *Boston Record Commissioners' Report,* Vol. XVIII, pp. 94-108.

40. *Debates and Proceedings in the Convention of the Commonwealth of Massachusetts, Held in the Year 1788* (Boston: William White, 1856), pp. 86, 266, February 6, 1788; see also William V.

Wells, *The Life and Public Service of Samuel Adams* (Boston: Little, Brown, & Co., 1865), Vol. III, p. 267.

41. Fisher Ames, *Works of Fisher Ames,* Seth Ames, editor (Boston: Little, Brown and Company, 1854), Vol. I, p. 54, to George Richards Minot on June 12, 1789.

42. *Debates and Other Proceedings of the Convention of Virginia,* David Robertson, editor (Richmond: Ritchie & Worsley and Augustine Davis, 1805), p. 275, Patrick Henry on June 14, 1788; see also *The Debates in the Several State Conventions, on the Adoption of the Federal Constitution as Recommended by the General Convention at Philadelphia in 1787,* Jonathan Elliot, editor (Washington: Printed for the Editor, 1836), Vol. III, p. 386.

43. *Debates . . . of the Convention of Virginia,* p. 43, Patrick Henry on June 5, 1788; see also Elliot's *Debates,* Vol. III, p. 45.

44. John Jay, *The Correspondence and Public Papers of John Jay,* Henry P. Johnston, editor (New York: G. P. Putnam's Sons, 1893), Vol. IV, p. 419, to John Murray, Jun., on April 15, 1818.

45. Jefferson, *Memoir, Correspondence, and Miscellanies,* Vol. II, p. 268, to Colonel Smith on November 13, 1787.

46. Thomas Jefferson, *The Works of Thomas Jefferson,* Paul L. Ford, editor (New York: G. P. Putnam's Sons, 1904), Vol. II, p. 180, from Jefferson's proposed Constitution for Virginia, June 1776.

47. *Debates . . . of the Convention of Virginia,* p. 461, Zechariah Johnson on June 25, 1788; see also Elliot's *Debates,* Vol. III, p. 646.

48. Richard Henry Lee, *An Additional Number Of Letters From The Federal Farmer To The Republican* (New York: 1788), p. 170, Letter XVIII, January 25, 1788.

49. Alexander Hamilton, John Jay, and James Madison, *The Federalist on the New Constitution* (Philadelphia: Benjamin Warner, 1818), p. 259, Federalist No. 46 by James Madison.

50. *Debates . . . of the Convention of Virginia,* p. 270, George Mason on June 14, 1788; see also Elliot's *Debates,* Vol. III, p. 380.

51. *Debates . . . of the Convention of Virginia,* p. 271, George Mason on June 14, 1788; see also Elliot's *Debates,* Vol. III, p. 381.

52. Thomas Paine, *The Writings of Thomas Paine,* Moncure Daniel Conway, editor (New York: G. P. Putnam's Sons, 1894), Vol. I, p. 55, from "Thoughts on Defensive War," *Pennsylvania Magazine,* July, 1775.

53. Paine, *Writings,* Vol. I, p. 56, from "Thoughts on Defensive War," *Pennsylvania Magazine,* July, 1775.

54. Elliot's *Debates,* Vol. IV, p. 442, Edmund Randolph in the House of Representatives on January 5, 1800.

55. *Debates . . . of Massachusetts, Held in the Year 1788,* p. 198, Theodore Sedgwick on January 24, 1788; see also Elliot's *Debates,* Vol. II, p. 97.

56. George Washington, *The Writings of George Washington,* Jared Sparks, editor (Boston: Ferdinand Andrews, 1838), Vol. XII, p. 8, from his First Annual Address to Congress on January 8, 1790.

57. George Washington, *Writings of George Washington,* John C. Fitzpatrick, editor (Washington, D. C.: U. S. Government Printing Office, 1931), Vol. II, p. 501, letter to George Mason on April 5, 1769.

58. Noah Webster, *An Examination into the Principles of the Federal Constitution Proposed by the Late Convention Held at Philadelphia* (Philadelphia: Prichard & Hall, 1787), p. 32.

59. Simon Gardner, *Observations on National Defense, Drawn from Capt. Partridge's Lecture on that Subject and from Gen. Sumner's Letter to the Venerable John Adams on the Importance of the Militia System* (Boston: Simon Gardner, 1824), p. iv.

60. *The Statutes at Large: Being A Collection of All the Laws of Virginia from the First Session of the Legislature, in the Year 1619,* William Waller Hening, editor (New York: For the editor, 1823), Vol. I, p. 127.

61. *The Statutes . . . of Virginia* (1823), Vol. I, pp. 127, 173-174, Act XLVIII and Act LI; see also Vol. II, p. 333 (1675-1676).

62. *The Right to Keep and Bear Arms,* United States Senate, p. 5; see also *The Statutes . . . of Virginia* (1823), Vol. II, pp. 304-305, Act II (1673); see also Vol. I, p. 525, Act XXV (1658-1659).

63. *The Statutes . . . of Virginia* (1823), Vol. II, p. 386.

64. *The Compact with the Charter and Laws of The Colony of New Plymouth,* William Brigham, editor (Boston: Dutton and Wentworth, 1836), pp. 44-45.

65. *The Compact . . . of New Plymouth,* p. 76.

66. *Records of the Colony of Rhode Island and Providence Plantations in New England,* J. Bartlett, editor (Providence: 1856), Vol. I, p. 94 (1639).

67. *The Code of 1650, Being a Compilation of the Earliest Laws and Orders of the General Court of Connecticut* (Hartford: Silus Andrus, 1830), p. 73.

68. *Statutes, Colonial and Revolutionary, 1768 to [1805],* Volume 19 of the Colonial Records of the State of Georgia, Allen D. Candler, editor (Atlanta: C. P. Byrd, State Printer, 1911), Vol. I, p. 137.

69. Lee, *Additional Letters,* p. 169, Letter XVIII, January 25, 1788.

70. Lee, *Additional Letters,* pp. 169-170, Letter XVIII, January 25, 1788.

71. Tench Coxe, *An Examination of the Constitution of the United States of America, Submitted to the People by the General Convention at Philadelphia, the 17th Day of September, 1787, and Since Adopted and Ratified by the Conventions of Eleven States* (Philadelphia: Zechariah Poulson, 1788), p. 21.

72. Samuel Adams, *Writings,* Vol. III, p. 251, to James Warren on January 7, 1776.

73. *Debates . . . of the Convention of Virginia,* p. 302, George Mason on June 16, 1788; see also Elliot's *Debates,* Vol. III, p. 425 (Elliot's incorrectly lists the date as June 14; it is properly June 16).

74. *An Abridgment of The Laws of The United States,* William Graydon, editor (Harrisburg: John Wyeth, 1803), p. 293, An Act of May 8, 1792.

75. *United States Code,* title 10, § 311(a).

76. Alabama Constitution (1867), art. 10, § 1.

77. Alabama Constitution (1875), art. 11, § 1.

78. Arkansas Constitution (1868), art. 11, § 1.

79. Arkansas Constitution (1874), art. 11, § 1.

80. Colorado Constitution (1876), art. 17, § 1.

81. Florida Constitution (1868), art. 12, § 1.

82. Florida Constitution (1885), art. 14, § 1.

83. Georgia Constitution (1868), art. 8, § 1.

84. Idaho Constitution (1889), art. 14, § 1.

85. Illinois Constitution (1818), art. 8, § 1.

86. Illinois Constitution (1870), art. 12, § 1.

87. Indiana Constitution (1851), art. 12, § 1.

88. Iowa Constitution (1846), art. 6, § 1.

89. Kansas Constitution (1855), art. 10, § 1.

90. Iowa Constitution (1857), art. 6, § 1.

91. Kansas Constitution (1857), art. 13, § 1.

92. Kansas Constitution (1858), art. 9, § 2.

93. Kansas Constitution (1859), art. 8, § 1

94. Kentucky Constitution (1850), art. 7, § 1.

95. Kentucky Constitution (1890), § 219.

96. Louisiana Constitution (1868), title. 8, art. 144.

97. Maine Constitution (1819), art. 7, § 5.

98. Maryland Constitution (1864), art. 9, § 1.

99. Michigan Constitution (1850), art. 17, § 1.

100. Mississippi Constitution (1868), art. 9, § 1.

101. Mississippi Constitution (1890), art. 9, § 214.

102. Missouri Constitution (1861).

103. Missouri Constitution (1865), art. 10, § 1.

104. Missouri Constitution (1875), art. 13, § 1.

105. Montana Constitution (1889), art. 14, § 1.

106. New York Constitution (1894), art. 11, § 1.

107. North Carolina Constitution (1868), art. 12, § 1.

108. North Carolina Constitution (1876), art. 12, § 1.

109. North Dakota Constitution (1889), art. 13, § 188.

110. Ohio Constitution (1851), art. 9, § 1.

111. Oregon Constitution (1857), art. 10, § 1.

112. South Carolina Constitution (1868), art. 13, § 1.

113. South Carolina Constitution (1895), art. 13, § 1.

114. South Dakota Constitution (1889), art. 15, § 1.

115. Utah Constitution (1895), art. 15, § 1.

116. Virginia Constitution (1870), art. 9, § 1.

117. Washington Constitution (1889), art. 10, § 1.

118. Wyoming Constitution (1889), art. 17, § 1.

119. James Madison, *The Papers of James Madison,* Henry D. Gilpin, editor (Washington: Langtree and O'Sullivan, 1840), Vol. III, pp. 1565-1566, September 12, 1787; see also *Records of the Federal Convention of 1787,* Max Farrand, editor (New Haven: Yale University Press, 1911), Vol. II, pp. 587-588, 637.

120. Elliot's *Debates,* Vol. I, p. 306, September 12, 1787.

121. *Debates . . . of the Convention of Virginia,* pp. 466-469, June 25, 1788; see also Elliot's *Debates,* Vol. III, pp. 652-655.

122. *Debates . . . of Massachusetts, Held in the Year 1788,* pp. 176-181, January 23, 1788; see also Elliot's *Debates,* Vol. II, pp. 87-92.

123. Joseph B. Walker, *A History of the New Hampshire Convention* (Boston: Cupples & Hurd, 1888), pp. 41-43, June 21, 1788.

124. Elliot's *Debates,* Vol. II, pp. 412-413, July 26, 1788.

125. *Collections of the Rhode Island Historical Society* (Providence: Knowles and Vose, 1843), Vol. V, pp. 320-321, March 24, 1788.

126. Elliot's *Debates,* Vol. IV, pp. 242-251, August 1-2, 1788.

127. *Annals of Congress; The Debates and Proceedings in the Congress of the United States* (Washington: Gales and Seaton, 1834), Vol. 1, p. 464, Elbridge Gerry on June 8, 1789.

128. Walker, *A History of the New Hampshire Convention,* p. 51, New Hampshire's proposals for a Bill of Rights, June 21, 1788; see also Elliot's *Debates,* Vol. I, p. 326.

129. *Debates . . . of Massachusetts, Held in the Year 1788,* p. 86, Samuel Adams, his constitutional amendment proposed during the Massachusetts ratification debates on February 6, 1788.

130. *The Address and Reasons of Dissent of the Minority of the Convention of Pennsylvania to their Constituents* (Boston: Powers, 1787), p. 6; see also *The Pennsylvania Packet, and Daily Advertiser,* December 18, 1787.

131. *Debates . . . of the Convention of Virginia,* pp. 470-473, Virginia's proposals for a Bill of Rights, June 27, 1788 (see also Elliot's *Debates,* Vol. III, p. 369); Elliot's *Debates,* Vol. I, p. 328, New York's proposals

for a Bill of Rights, July 26, 1788; and Elliot's *Debates*, Vol. I, p. 335, Rhode Island's proposals for a Bill of Rights, May 29, 1790.

132. Albert Gallatin, *The Papers of Albert Gallatin* (Philadelphia: Historic Publications, c. 1969), microform, to Alexander Addison on October 7, 1789.

133. *Independent Chronicle* (Boston), February 22, 1787, Fisher Ames writing as Camillus.

134. Jefferson, *Works* (1904), Vol. V, pp. 371-372, to James Madison on December 20, 1787.

135. James Madison, *Letters and Other Writings of James Madison, Fourth President of the United States* (New York: R. Worthington, 1884), Vol. I, p. 423, to Thomas Jefferson on October 17, 1788.

136. *Annals of Congress; The Debates and Proceedings* (1834), Vol. 1, pp. 450, 454, 458, James Madison on June 8, 1789.

137. *Annals of Congress; The Debates and Proceedings* (1834), Vol. 1, p. 451, James Madison on June 8, 1789.

138. Delaware Constitution (1792), Preamble.

139. Delaware Constitution (1831), Preamble.

140. South Carolina Constitution (1868), art. I, § 1.

141. Arkansas Constitution (1836), art. 2, § 1.

142. Arkansas Constitution (1874), art. 2, § 2.

143. California Constitution (1849), art. I, § 1.

144. Colorado Constitution (1876), art. 2, § 3.

145. Florida Constitution (1838), art. I, § 1.

146. Florida Constitution (1868), art. I, § 1.

147. Florida Constitution (1885), § 1.

148. Idaho Constitution (1889), art. I, § 1.

149. Illinois Constitution (1818), art. 8, § 1.

150. Indiana Constitution (1816), art. I, § 1.

151. Iowa Constitution (1820), art. 2, § 1.

152. Kansas Constitution (1855), art. I, § 1.

153. Maine Constitution (1819), art. I, § 1.

154. Massachusetts Constitution (1780), art. I, § 1.

155. Nevada Constitution (1864), art. I, § 1.

156. New Hampshire Constitution (1783), art. 1, § 2.

157. New Hampshire Constitution (1792), part I, art. 2.
158. New Hampshire Constitution (1902), part 1, § 2.
159. New Jersey Constitution (1844), art. I, § 1.
160. North Dakota Constitution (1889), art. I, § 1.
161. Pennsylvania Constitution (1776), art. 1.
162. Pennsylvania Constitution (1790), art. 9, § 1.
163. South Dakota Constitution (1889), art. 6, § 1.
164. Utah Constitution (1895), art. 1, § 1.
165. Vermont Constitution (1777), chapter 1, § 1.
166. Colorado Constitution (1876), art. 2, § 13.
167. Mississippi Constitution (1890), art. 3, § 12.
168. Missouri Constitution (1875), art. 1, § 17.
169. Montana Constitution (1889), art. 3, § 13.
170. Idaho Constitution (1889), art. 1, § 11.
171. Kansas Constitution (1855), art. 1, § 4.
172. Utah Constitution (1895), art. 1, § 6.
173. Alabama Constitution (1819), art. 1, § 23.
174. Alabama Constitution (1865), art. 1, § 27.
175. Alabama Constitution (1875), art. 1, § 27.
176. Alabama Constitution (1901), art. 1, § 26.
177. Connecticut Constitution (1818), art. 1, § 17.
178. Florida Constitution (1868), art. 1, § 22.
179. Florida Constitution (1885), § 20.
180. Indiana Constitution (1816), art. 1, § 20.
181. Indiana Constitution (1851), art. 1, § 32.
182. Michigan Constitution (1835), art. 1, § 13.
183. Michigan Constitution (1850), art. 18, § 7.
184. Mississippi Constitution (1817), art. 1, § 23.
185. Mississippi Constitution (1833), art. 1, § 23.
186. Ohio Constitution (1802), § 20.
187. Oregon Constitution (1857), art. 1, § 28.
188. Pennsylvania Constitution (1776), § 13.
189. Texas Constitution (1838), § 14.
190. Texas Constitution (1845), art. 1, § 13.
191. Vermont Constitution (1777), chapter 1, § 15.

192. Vermont Constitution (1793), art. 16.

193. Georgia Constitution (1865), art. 1, § 4.

194. Georgia Constitution (1877), art. 1, § 1, part 22.

195. Kentucky Constitution (1799), § 23.

196. Kentucky Constitution (1850), § 25.

197. Missouri Constitution (1820), art. 13. § 3.

198. Pennsylvania Constitution (1790), § 21.

199. South Dakota Constitution (1889), art. 6, § 24.

200. Vermont Constitution (1786), chapter 1, § 18.

201. Vermont Constitution (1793), chapter 1, art. 16.

202. Washington Constitution (1889), art. 1 § 24.

203. Wyoming Constitution (1889), art. 1, § 24.

204. *Trop v. Dulles,* 356 U.S. 86, 101 (1958).

205. *Independent Chronicle* (Boston), January 21, 1796, Sam Adams to the legislature of Massachusetts on January 19, 1796.

206. George Washington, *Address of George Washington, President of the United States . . . Preparatory to His Declination* (Baltimore: George and Henry S. Keatinge, 1796), p. 22.

207. Alexander Hamilton, *Works* (1851), Vol. VI, p. 542, to James Bayard, April, 1802.

208. Joseph Story, *A Discourse Pronounced Upon the Inauguration of the Author, as Dane Professor of Law in Harvard University on the Twenty-Fifth Day of August, 1829* (Boston: Hilliard, Gray, Little, and Wilkins, 1829), p. 14.

209. Jefferson, *Writings* (1904), Vol. XV, p. 277, to William Charles Jarvis on September 28, 1820.

210. Charles C. Jones, *Biographical Sketches of the Delegates from Georgia to the Continental Congress* (Boston: Houghton, Mifflin and Company, 1891), p. 7.

211. John Quincy Adams, *Letters of John Quincy Adams to His Son on the Bible and its Teachings* (Auburn: James M. Alden, 1850), p. 62.

212. Jefferson, *Memoir, Correspondence, and Miscellanies* (1830), Vol. III, p. 509, from Jefferson's "Syllabus of an Estimate of the Merit of the Doctrines of Jesus Compared with Those of Others," to Dr. Benjamin Rush on April 21, 1803.

213. John Adams, *Works* (1854), Vol. IX, p. 229, to the Officers of the First Brigade of the Third Division of the Militia of Massachusetts on October 11, 1798.

214. John Quincy Adams, *Letters . . . to His Son on the Bible and its Teachings,* pp. 22-23.

215. Wells, *The Life and Public Service of Samuel Adams,* Vol. I, p. 22, quoting from a political essay by Samuel Adams published in *The Public Advertiser,* 1748.

216. Jones, *Biographical Sketches,* pp. 6-7.

217. *Connecticut Courant,* June 7, 1802, p. 3, Oliver Ellsworth, to the General Assembly of the State of Connecticut Now in Session.

218. Bernard C. Steiner, *One Hundred and Ten Years of Bible Society Work in Maryland, 1810-1920* (Baltimore: The Maryland Bible Society, 1921), p. 14.

219. Benjamin Rush, *Letters of Benjamin Rush,* L. H. Butterfield, editor (Princeton: Princeton University Press, for the American Philosophical Society, 1951), Vol. I, p. 505, "To American Farmers About to Settle in New Parts of the United States," March 1789.

220. George Washington, *Address . . . Preparatory to His Declination,* p. 23.

221. Daniel Webster, *Mr. Webster's Address at the Laying of the Cornerstone of the Addition to the Capitol, July 4, 1851* (Washington: Gideon and Co., 1851), p. 23.

222. Noah Webster, *A Collection of Essays and Fugitiv [sic] Writings on Moral, Historical, Political, and Literary Subjects* (Boston: Isaiah Thomas and E. T. Andrews, 1790), p. 22, from his "On the Education of Youth in America, 1788."

223. John Witherspoon, *The Works of John Witherspoon* (Edinburgh: J. Ogle, 1815), Vol. VII, pp. 118-119, from his Lectures on Moral Philosophy, Lecture 14, on Jurisprudence.

224. Robert Winthrop, *Addresses and Speeches on Various Occasions* (Boston: Little, Brown and Co., 1852), p. 172, from an Address Delivered at the Annual Meeting of the Massachusetts Bible Society in Boston, May 28, 1849.

225. Daniel Webster, *Works of Daniel Webster* (Boston: Little, Brown and Company, 1853), Vol. I, pp. 41-42, from a speech at Plymouth on December 22, 1820.

226. Benjamin Rush, *Essays, Literary, Moral and Philosophical* (Philadelphia: Thomas and Samuel Bradford, 1798), p. 112, from his "Defense of the Use of the Bible as a School Book, March 10, 1781."

227. *Debates . . . of the Convention of Virginia,* p. 43, Patrick Henry on June 9, 1788; see also Elliot's *Debates,* Vol. III, p. 168.

228. Lee, *Additional Letters,* p. 170, Letter XVIII, January 25, 1788.

229. Jefferson, *Writings* (1903), Vol. V, p. 85, to Peter Carr on August 19, 1785.

230. John Quincy Adams, *Memoirs of John Quincy Adams, Comprising Portions of his Diary from 1795 to 1848,* Charles Francis Adams, editor (Philadelphia: J. B. Lippincott & Co., 1874), Vol. III, p. 497, to Thomas Boylston Adams, in a letter on September 8, 1810.

231. John Quincy Adams, *Memoirs,* Vol. I, p. 5, to Mr. Sturge, 1846.

232. John Quincy Adams, *Memoirs,* Vol. I, pp. 5-6, to Mr. Sturge, 1846.

233. John Quincy Adams, *Memoirs,* Vol. VII, p. 325, on August 20, 1827.

234. William H. Seward, *John Quincy Adams, Life and Public Services of John Quincy Adams, Sixth President of the United States, with The Eulogy Delivered Before the Legislature of New York* (Auburn: Derby, Miller and Company, 1849), p. 323.

235. James Kent, *Memoirs and Letters of James Kent,* William Kent, editor (Boston: Little, Brown, and Company, 1898), p. 123.

Bibliography

Books

[An] Abridgement of the Laws of the United States, or, A Complete Digest of all Such Acts of Congress as Concern the United States at Large. William Graydon, editor. Harrisburg: John Wyeth, 1803.

Adams, John. *The Works of John Adams, Second President of the United States: With a Life of the Author, Notes and Illustrations.* Charles Francis Adams, editor. Boston: Charles C. Little and James Brown, 1850-1856. Ten volumes.

Adams, John Quincy. *An Oration Delivered Before the Cincinnati Astronomical Society on the Occasion of Laying the Cornerstone of an Astronomical Observatory on the 10th of November, 1843.* Cincinnati: Shepard & Co., 1843.

Adams, John Quincy. *Letters of John Quincy Adams to His Son on the Bible and Its Teachings.* Auburn: James M. Alden, 1850.

Adams, John Quincy. *Memoirs of John Quincy Adams. Comprising Portions of His Diary from 1795 to 1848.* Charles Francis Adams, editor. Philadelphia: J. B. Lippincott and Company, 1874-1877. Twelve volumes.

Adams, Samuel. *Writings of Samuel Adams*, Harry Alonzo Cushing, editor. New York: G. P. Putnam's Sons, 1904-1908. Four volumes.

Address and Reasons of Dissent of the Minority of the Convention of Pennsylvania to their Constituents. Boston: Powers, 1787.

Ames, Fisher. *Works of Fisher Ames with a Selection from his Speeches and Correspondence.* Seth Ames editor. Boston: Little, Brown and Company, 1854. Two volumes.

Annals of Congress; Debates and Proceedings in the Congress of the United States. Washington: Gales and Seaton, 1834.

Blackstone, William. *Commentaries on the Laws of England*. Philadelphia: Robert Bell, 1769-1771. Four volumes.

Blackstone's Commentaries: With Notes and Reference, to the Constitution of the United States; and of the Commonwealth of Virginia. St. George Tucker, editor. Philadelphia: William Young Birch, and Abraham Small, 1803. Five volumes.

[The] Code of 1650, Being a Compilation of the Earliest Laws and Orders of the General Court of Connecticut. Hartford: Silus Andrus, 1830.

Collections of the Rhode Island Historical Society. Providence: Knowles and Vose, 1827-1867. Six volumes.

[The] Compact with the Charter and Laws of the Colony of New Plymouth: together with the charter of the council at Plymouth. William Brigham, editor. Boston: Dutton and Wentworth, 1836.

Coxe, Tench. *An Examination of the Constitution of the United States of America, Submitted to the People by the General Convention at Philadelphia, the 17th Day of September, 1787, and Since Adopted and Ratified by the Conventions of Eleven States*. Philadelphia: Zechariah Poulson, 1788.

Debates and Other Proceedings of the Convention of Virginia, Convened at Richmond, on Monday the Second Day of June, 1788, for the Purpose of Deliberating on the Constitution Recommended by the Grand Federal Convention. David Robertson, editor. Richmond: Ritchie & Worsley and Augustine Davis, 1805.

Debates and Proceedings in the Convention of the Commonwealth of Massachusetts, Held in the Year 1788, and which Finally Ratified the Constitution of the United States. Boston: William White, 1856.

Debates in Several State Conventions, on the Adoption of the Federal Constitution as Recommended by the General Convention at Philadelphia in 1787. Together with the Journal of the Federal Convention, Luther Martins's letter, Yates's Minutes, Congressio-

nal Opinions, Virginia and Kentucky Resolutions of '98-'99, and Other Illustrations of the Constitution. Jonathan Elliot, editor. Washington, D. C.: Printed for the Editor, 1836. Four volumes.

Dickinson, John. *Letters from a Farmer in Pennsylvania.* R. T. H. Halsey, editor. New York: The Outlook Company. 1903.

Encyclopedia of Religious Quotations. Frank Mead, editor. New Jersey: Fleming H. Revell Company, 1965.

Gallatin, Albert. *Papers of Albert Gallatin.* Philadelphia: Historic Publications, c. 1969. Microform.

Gardner, Simon. *Observations on National Defense Drawn from Capt. Partridge's Lecture on that Subject and from Gen. Sumner's Letter to the Venerable John Adams on the Importance of the Militia System.* Boston: Simon Gardner, 1824.

Hamilton, Alexander. *The Farmer Refuted: Or, A More Impartial and Comprehensive View of the Dispute Between Great Britain and the Colonies.* New York: James Rivington, 1775.

Hamilton, Alexander, John Jay, and James Madison. *The Federalist on the New Constitution;* written in 1788. Philadelphia: Benjamin Warner, 1818.

Jay, John. *Correspondence and Public Papers of John Jay First Chief-Justice of the United States, Member and President of the Continental Congress, Minister to Spain, Member of Commission to Negotiate Treaty of Independence, Envoy to Great Britain, Governor of New York, etc. 1794-1826.* Henry P. Johnston, editor. New York: G. P. Putnam's Sons, 1890-1893. Four volumes.

Jefferson, Thomas. *Memoir, Correspondence, and Miscellanies from the Papers of Thomas Jefferson.* Thomas Jefferson Randolph, editor. Boston: Gray and Bowen, 1830. Four volumes.

Jefferson, Thomas. *Works of Thomas Jefferson.* Paul L. Ford, editor. New York: G. P. Putnam's Sons, 1904-1905. Twelve volumes.

Jefferson, Thomas. *Writings of Thomas Jefferson.* Albert Bergh, editor. Washington, D.C.: Thomas Jefferson Memorial Association, 1903-1904. Twenty volumes.

Jones, Charles C. *Biographical Sketches of the Delegates from Georgia to the Continental Congress.* Boston: Houghton, Mifflin and Company, 1891.

Kent, James. *Commentaries on American Law.* New York: O. Halsted, 1826-1830. Four volumes.

Kent, James. *Memoirs and Letters of James Kent, LL. D. Late Chancellor of the State of New York. Author of "Commentaries on American Law," etc.* William Kent, editor. Boston: Little, Brown and Company, 1898.

Lee, Richard Henry. *An Additional Number of Letters From the Federal Farmer to the Republican Leading to a Fair Examination of the System of Government Proposed by the Late Convention; to Several Essential and Necessary Alterations in it; and Calculated to Illustrate and Support the Principles and Positions Laid Down in the Preceding Letters [together with] Observations on the New Constitution, and on the Federal and State Conventions by a Columbian Patriot.* New York: 1788.

Madison, James. *Letters and Other Writings of James Madison, Fourth President of the United States.* New York: R. Worthington, 1884. Four volumes.

Madison, James. *Papers of James Madison Purchased by Order of Congress; Being His Correspondence and Reports of Debates During the Congress of The Confederation and the Reports of Debates in the Federal Convention.* Henry D. Gilpin, editor. Washington: Langtree and O'Sullivan, 1840. Three volumes.

Madison, James. *Selections from the Private Correspondence of James Madison from 1813-1836.* J. C. McGuire, editor. Washington, 1853.

Paine, Thomas. *Writings of Thomas Paine.* Moncure Daniel Conway, editor. New York: G. P. Putnam's Sons, 1894-1896. Twelve volumes.

Rawle, William. *A View of the Constitution of the United States of America.* Philadelphia: Philip H. Nicklin, 1829.

Records of the Colony of Rhode Island and Providence Plantations in New England. J. Bartlett, editor. Providence: 1856-1865. Ten volumes.

Records of the Federal Convention of 1787. Max Farrand, editor. New Haven: Yale University Press, 1911. Three volumes.

Rush, Benjamin. *Essays, Literary, Moral and Philosophical.* Philadelphia: Thomas and Samuel F. Bradford, 1798.

Rush, Benjamin. *Letters of Benjamin Rush.* L. H. Butterfield, editor. Princeton: Princeton University Press for the American Philosophical Society, 1951. Two volumes.

Seward, William H. *Life and Public Services of John Quincy Adams, Sixth President of the United States, with the Eulogy Delivered Before the Legislature of New York.* Auburn: Derby, Miller and Company, 1849.

Statutes at Large: Being A Collection of All the Laws of Virginia from the First Session of the Legislature, in the Year 1619. William Waller Hening, editor. New York: Printed for the Editor, 1823. Thirteen volumes.

Statutes, Colonial and Revolutionary, 1768 to [1805]. Volume 19 of the Colonial Records of the State of Georgia. Atlanta: C. P. Byrd, State Printer, 1911. Two volumes.

Steiner, Bernard C. *One Hundred and Ten Years of Bible Society Work in Maryland, 1810-1920.* Baltimore: The Maryland Bible Society, 1921.

Story, Joseph. *Commentaries on the Constitution of the United States; with a Preliminary Review of the Constitutional History of the Colonies and States, before the Adoption of the Constitution.* Boston: Hilliard, Gray and Company, 1833. Three volumes.

Story, Joseph. *Discourse Pronounced Upon the Inauguration of the Author, as Dane Professor of Law in Harvard University on the Twenty-fifth Day of August, 1829.* Boston: Hilliard, Gray, Little, and Wilkins, 1829.

Swift, Zephaniah. *A System of the Laws of the State of Connecticut.* Windham: John Byrne, 1795-1796. Two volumes.

Tucker, Henry St. George. *A Few Lectures on Natural Law.* Charlottesville: James Alexander, 1844.

Tucker, John Randolph. *Constitution of the United States. A Critical Discussion of its Genesis, Development, and Interpretation.* Henry St. George Tucker, ed. Chicago: Callaghan & Co., 1899. 2 vol.

Walker, Joseph B. *A History of the New Hampshire Convention for the Investigation, Discussion, and Decision of the Federal Constitution: and of the Old North Meeting-House of Concord, in which it was Ratified by the Ninth State, and thus Rendered Operative, at One O'clock P.M., on Saturday, the 21st Day of June, 1788.* Boston: Cupples & Hurd, 1888.

Washington, George. *Address of George Washington, President of the United States, and Late Commander in Chief of the American Army, to the People of the United States, Preparatory to His Declination.* Baltimore: George and Henry S. Keatinge, 1796.

Washington, George. *Writings of George Washington; being his Correspondence, Addresses, Messages, and other Papers, Official and Private, Selected and Published from the Original Manuscripts with a Life of the Author, Notes and Illustrations.* Jared Sparks, editor. Boston: Ferdinand Andrews, 1834-1838. Twelve volumes.

Washington, George. *Writings of Washington.* John C. Fitzpatrick, editor. Washington, D. C.: U.S. Government Printing Office, 1931-1944. Thirty-nine volumes.

Webster, Daniel. *Mr. Webster's Address at the Laying of the Cornerstone of the Addition to the Capitol, July 4, 1851.* Washington: Gideon and Co., 1851.

Webster, Daniel. *Works of Daniel Webster.* Boston: Little, Brown and Company, 1853. Six volumes.

Webster, Noah. *A Collection of Essays and Fugitiv [sic] Writings on Moral, Historical, Political, and Literary Subjects.* Boston: Isaiah Thomas and E. T. Andrews, 1790.

Webster, Noah. *An Examination into the Principles of the Federal Constitution Proposed by the Late Convention Held at Philadelphia. With Answers to the Principle Objections that have been Raised Against the System.* Philadelphia: Prichard & Hall, 1787.

Webster, Noah. *The Holy Bible, Containing the Old and New Testaments, in the Common Version. With Amendments of the Language.* New Haven: Durrie & Peck, 1833.

Wells, William V. *Life and Public Services of Samuel Adams, Being A Narrative of his Acts and Opinions, and of his Agency in Producing and Forwarding the American Revolution.* Boston: Little, Brown & Co., 1865. Three volumes.

Wilson, James. *The Works of the Honorable James Wilson, L.L.D. Late One of the Associate Justices of the Supreme Court of the United States and Professor of Law in the College of Philadelphia.* Bird Wilson, editor. Philadelphia: Bronson and Chauncey, 1804. Three volumes.

Wilson, James, Thomas McKean. *Commentaries on the Constitution of the United States of America, with that Constitution Prefixed, in which are Unfolded the Principles of Free Government and the Superior Advantages of Republicanism Demonstrated.* London: J. Debrett, 1792.

Winthrop, Robert. *Addresses and Speeches on Various Occasions.* Boston: Little, Brown and Co., 1852.

Witherspoon, John. *The Works of John Witherspoon, D. D. Sometime Minister of the Gospel at Paisley, and Late President of Princeton College, in New Jersey. Containing Essays, Sermons, &c. on Important Subjects Intended to Illustrate and Establish the Doctrine of Salvation by Grace, and to Point Out its Influence on Holiness of Life. Together with his Lectures on Moral Philosophy, Eloquence and Divinity; His Speeches in the American Congress, and Many Other Valuable Pieces, Never Before Published in this Country.* Edinburgh: J. Ogle, 1815. Ten volumes.

Articles

Adams, John. "On Private Revenge," *Boston Gazette*, September 5, 1763.

Benedetto, Richard. "Gun Rights Are A Myth," *USA Today*, December 28, 1994.

Gartner, Michael, former president of NBC News. USA Today, January 16, 1992.

Henigan, Dennis. "The Right To Be Armed: A Constitutional Illusion," *The San Francisco Barrister*, December, 1989.

"A History of the Second Amendment," *Austin American Statesman*, April 3, 2000.

"Legal Guns Kill Too," *The Washington Post*, November 5, 1999.

Paine, Thomas. "Thoughts on Defensive War," *Pennsylvania Magazine*, July, 1775.

"Time for Gun Control," *New York Post*, August 12, 1999.

Documents/Legal References

ACLU. Policy Statement #47, 1996.

Brief for an Ad Hoc Group of [Fifty-Two] Law Professors and Historians as Amici Curiae, *United States v. Timothy Joe Emerson* (5th Cir. 1999) (No. 99-10331).

Trop v. Dulles, Secretary of State, et al. 356 U.S. 86 (1958).

United States Senate, Subcommittee on the Constitution of the Committee of the Judiciary. *The Right to Keep and Bear Arms*. Ninety-Seventh Congress, Second Session, February, 1982.

Periodicals

Connecticut Courant, June 7, 1802.

Independent Chronicle (Boston), February 22, 1787.

Independent Chronicle (Boston), January 21, 1796.

[The] Pennsylvania Packet and Daily Advertiser, December 18, 1787.

WallBuilders
Featured Product

Battle of Lexington Print

This museum-quality print features W.B. Wollen's depiction of the Battle of Lexington (a portion of which is shown on the cover of this book). Suitable for framing (18 x 24) and printed on acid-free paper.

Battle of Lexington Print   (PR01) $9.95

The Battle of Lexington
April 19, 1775 • By W.B. Wollen, 1905 • Reproduced by WallBuilders, (800) 873-2845

Also Available from WallBuilders

A history curriculum that unabashedly delivers the truth!
Drive Through History America
written by David Barton & presented by award-winning actor Dave Stotts

Visit our website for other great resources!

800-873-2845 • www.wallbuilders.com